New Reflections for Advent

the columba press

First published in 2011 by
the columba press
55A Spruce Avenue, Stillorgan Industrial Park,
Blackrock, Co Dublin

Cover designed by Bill Bolger
Origination by The Columba Press
Printed in Ireland by Gemini International Ltd

ISBN 978-1-85607-752-1

Copyright © 2012, Donal Neary SJ

Contents

Introduction	6
1st Sunday of Advent A	8
1st Sunday of Advent B	10
1st Sunday of Advent C	12
Monday Week 1	14
Tuesday Week 1	16
Wednesday Week 1	18
Thursday Week 1	20
Saturday Week 122	24
2nd Sunday of Advent A	26
2nd Sunday of Advent B	28
2nd Sunday of Advent C	30
Monday Week 2	32
Tuesday Week 2	34
Wednesday Week 2	36
Thursday Week 2	38
Friday Week 2	40
Saturday Week 2	42
3rd Sunday of Advent A	44
4th Sunday of Advent B	46
5th Sunday of Advent C	48
Monday Week 3	50
Tuesday Week 3	52
Wednesday Week 3	54
Thursday Week 3	56

Friday Week 3	58
17 December	60
18 December	62
19 December	64
20 December	66
3rd Sunday of Advent A	68
3rd Sunday of Advent B	68
3rd Sunday of Advent C	72
22 December	74
23 December	76
17 December	78
17 December	80
17 December	82

Introduction

Pope Benedict wrote: 'Advent is concerned with that very connection between memory and hope which is so necessary. Advent's intention is to awaken the most profound and basic emotional memory within us, namely, the memory of the God who became a child. This is a healing memory; it brings hope. The purpose of the church's year is continually to rehearse her great history of memories, to awaken the heart's memory so that it can discern the star of hope … It is the beautiful task of Advent to awaken in all of us memories of goodness and thus to open doors of hope.'

New Reflections for Advent gives simple helps and reflections for prayer in the busy days coming up to Christmas. It's a time rich in insights about Christian faith, and invites us to allow Christmas happen gradually for the four weeks. The hurry of Christmas and its early start may harmonise little with the slow yet certain pace of Advent. Our hope is that this little book may help us recognise 'the star of hope', the beginnings of the new light of the world, Jesus Christ.

- Read the gospel, even aloud. Notice what strikes you and take that with you into the day. Make the prayer your own – add to it if you wish, and the reflection may link the gospel to prayer, faith and human living.
- The prayer for the day may be helpful, with adaptation where necessary, for school assemblies, parish liturgies, prayer groups, and other meetings where people find it useful to have some material to begin.

Donal Neary SJ

Many of the reflections have been used, with some adaptation and revision, on the website Sacred Space www.sacredspace.ie and published in Sacred Space: the prayer book *(2010 and 2011 editions), Michelle Anderson Publishing Pty Ltd, Melbourne, Australia, and used here with thanks and appreciation.*

7

1st Sunday of Advent: A

Matthew 24: 37-44
Jesus said to his disciples: 'But about that day and hour no one knows, neither the angels of heaven, nor the Son, but only the Father. For as the days of Noah were, so will be the coming of the Son of Man. For as in those days before the flood they were eating and drinking, marrying and giving in marriage, until the day Noah entered the ark, and they knew nothing until the flood came and swept them all away, so too will be the coming of the Son of Man. Then two will be in the field; one will be taken and one will be left. Two women will be grinding meal together; one will be taken and one will be left. Keep awake therefore, for you do not know on what day your Lord is coming. But understand this: if the owner of the house had known in what part of the night the thief was coming, he would have stayed awake and would not have let his house be broken into. Therefore you also must be ready, for the Son of Man is coming at an unexpected hour.'

Prayer

Be with me Lord when I need strength and healing in my life;
Be with your people so that we may follow you in loving service.
Be with our world in its need for your mercy and your care. Amen.

Reflection

The message of Christmas is that God loves us enough to become one of us; that we belong to each other as children of God; that God is poor. A suggestion that for these weeks we might select something for a week or a day to let these truths centre in the soul – thank God each day that he loves you; look on people and really believe that they are children of God especially those you find difficult; give something to the poor.

1st Sunday of Advent: B

Mark 13:33-73
Jesus said to his disciples: 'Beware, keep alert; for you do not know when the time will come. It is like a man going on a journey, when he leaves home and puts his slaves in charge, each with his work, and commands the doorkeeper to be on the watch. Therefore, keep awake – for you do not know when the master of the house will come, in the evening, or at midnight, or at cockcrow, or at dawn, or else he may find you asleep when he comes suddenly. And what I say to you I say to all: Keep awake.'

Prayer

Be with me Lord when I need strength and healing in my life;
Be with your people so that we follow you in loving service.
Be with our world in its need for your mercy and your care. Amen.

Reflection

Jesus' message and life was to make a difference and save the world. That's the call – to do the world a world of good. We need to believe that each of us can make a difference – in the family, the neighbourhood, the school. We deepen that conviction in many ways, and one way is to keep in touch with God in prayer. Advent can be that time – that we keep in touch with God, and through us God's grace and care can flow into our world.

1st Sunday of Advent: C

Jesus said to his disciples: 'As it was in Noah's day, so will it be when the Son of Man comes. For in those days before the Flood people were eating, drinking, taking wives, taking husbands, right up to the day Noah went into the Ark, and they suspected nothing till the Flood came and swept all away. It will be like this when the Son of Man comes. Then of two men in the field one is taken, one left; of two women at the millstone one is taken, one left.

'So stay awake, because you do not know the day when your master is coming. You may be quite sure of this that if the householder had known at what time of the night the burgler would come, he would have stayed awake and would not have allowed anyone to break through the wall of his house. Therefore, you too must stand ready because the Son of Man is coming at an hour you do not expect.'

Prayer

Be with me Lord when I need strength and healing in my life;
Be with your people so that we follow you in loving service.
Be with our world in its need for your mercy and your care. Amen.

Reflection

The best waitings like waiting for birth are slow. Parents wonder about their child who will he/she be like? Health? Mothers need support and love; children look forward to another baby; grand-parents wait in pride. Even when the family situation is limited, we wait in joy and hope for the child. Like Mary and Joseph, Elizabeth and Zechariah and all the bible parents who waited, often for many years. If we wait in faith and in hope, then everything, even the carols sung too early and the celebrations planned too early, can remind us of the God who is coming soon in Jesus Christ, to be born of Mary.

Monday Week 1

Matthew 8:5-11

When Jesus entered Capernaum, a centurion came to him, appealing to him and saying: 'Lord, my servant is lying at home paralysed, in terrible distress.' And he said to him: 'I will come and cure him.' The centurion answered: 'Lord, I am not worthy to have you come under my roof; but only speak the word, and my servant will be healed. For I also am a man under authority, with soldiers under me; and I say to one, 'Go ', and he goes, and to another, 'Come', and he comes, and to my slave, 'Do this ', and the slave does it.' When Jesus heard him, he was amazed and said to those who followed him: 'Truly I tell you, in no one in Israel have I found such faith. I tell you, many will come from east and west and will eat with Abraham and Isaac and Jacob in the kingdom of heaven.'

Prayer

Be with me Lord when I need strength and healing in my life;
Be with your people so that we may follow you in loving service.
Be with our world in its need for your mercy and your care. Amen.

Reflection

The beginning of a new year in the church sets the scene for a major message of Jesus, like his mission statement or policy document. Many more – a huge number – will take their place with the familiar holy people of Israel in the kingdom of God. The faith of a Roman soldier, a hated person for the local people, was the picture and sign of the coming of all nations into God's kingdom. Prayer humbles us to let us know that we are of these nations; getting into God's kingdom and love in his gracious gift and legacy. Advent is the month of the humble God, the child who is God.

Tuesday: Week 1

Luke 10:21-24
At that same hour Jesus rejoiced in the Holy Spirit and said: 'I thank you, Father, Lord of heaven and earth, because you have hidden these things from the wise and the intelligent and have revealed them to infants; yes, Father, for such was your gracious will. All things have who the Father is except the Son and anyone to whom the Son chooses to reveal him.' Then turning to the disciples, Jesus said to them privately: 'Blessed are the eyes that see what you see! For I tell you that many prophets and kings desired to see what you see, but did not see it, and to hear what you hear, but did not hear it.'

Prayer

Be with me Lord when I need strength and healing in my life;
Be with your people so that we may follow you in loving service.
Be with our world in its need for your mercy and your care. Amen.

Reflection

What have I learned in prayer? What things are hidden from the wise and the prudent that I have learnt in the heart of prayer? Can I think over the mystery of prayer in my life and wonder what it has done for me? How has prayer made me who I am? What have I 'seen' and 'heard' in prayer that I desired? Can I give thanks for all this?

Wednesday: Week 1

Matthew 15:29-37
After Jesus had left that place, he passed along the Sea of Galilee, and he went up the mountain, where he sat down. Great crowds came to him, bringing with them the lame, the maimed, the blind, the mute, and many others. They put them at his feet, and he cured them, so that the crowd was amazed when they saw the mute speaking, the maimed whole, the lame walking, and the blind seeing. And they praised the God of Israel. Then Jesus called his disciples to him and said: 'I have compassion for the crowd, because they have been with me now for three days and have nothing to eat; and I do not want to send them away hungry, for they might faint on the way.' The disciples said to him: 'Where are we to get enough bread in the desert to feed so great a crowd? ' Jesus asked them: 'How many loaves have you?' They said, 'Seven, and a few small fish.' Then ordering the crowd to sit down on the ground, he took the seven loaves and the fish; and after giving thanks he broke them and gave them to the disciples, and the disciples distributed them, as much as they wanted.

Prayer

Be with me Lord when I need strength and healing in my life;
Be with your people so that we may follow you in loving service.
Be with our world in its need for your mercy and your care. Amen.

Reflection

Things happened around Jesus. People got better, physically and spiritually. In this scene they are healed, fed and taught. Things happen when we pray. Prayer is journey to a new destination in ourselves, to the part of ourselves where we sing and dance, weep and laugh, cry and reach out to others in love and compassion and need. Prayer is an adventure. Time of prayer each day is a venture into the new and uncharted land of love of self, others and God.

Thursday: Week 1

Matthew 7:21, 24-27
Jesus said to the people: 'Not everyone who says to me, "Lord, Lord" will enter the kingdom of heaven, but only one who does the will of my Father in heaven. Everyone then who hears these words of mine and acts on them will be like a wise man who built his house on rock. The rain fell, the floods came, and the winds blew and beat on that house, but it did not fall, because it had been founded on rock. And everyone who hears these words of mine and does not act on them will be like a foolish man who built his house on sand. The rain fell, and the floods came, and the winds blew and beat against that house, and it fell and great was its fall.'

Prayer
Be with me Lord when I need strength and healing in my life;
Be with your people so that we follow you in loving service.
Be with our world in its need for your mercy and your care. Amen.

Reflection
There are many ways to 'hear' words. Just the sound, the external meaning, giving information or directions. The word of God is more like the word of a friend, spoken to the mind and heart. Or like the words of a caring parent giving advice or directions out of love. The word of God gives meaning to life and is spoken always in love. Prayer is giving time to hearing this word in the deepest levels of our heart.

Friday: Week 1

Matthew 9:27-31

As Jesus went on his way, two blind men followed him, crying loudly: 'Have mercy on us, Son of David!' When he entered the house, the blind men came to him; and Jesus said to them: 'Do you believe that I am able to do this?' They said to him: 'Yes, Lord.' Then he touched their eyes and said, 'According to your faith let it be done to you.' And their eyes were opened.

Prayer

Be with me Lord when I need strength and healing in my life;
Be with your people so that we may follow you in loving service.
Be with our world in its need for your mercy and your care. Amen.

Reflection

How could they follow him if they were blind? By hearing his voice, or maybe others led them to him. How did they know what to ask for? They knew they needed physical and spiritual sight, so they asked for more than sight – for mercy. Their faith in him opened their hearts to appeal to him. Their faith touched power in Jesus and they were healed. They knew their need – of God and of others , did not hide their need and were healed.

Saturday: Week 1

Matthew 9:35; 10:1:6-8

Jesus went about all the cities and villages, teaching in their synagogues, and proclaiming the good news of the kingdom, and curing every disease and every sickness. When he saw the crowds, he had compassion for them, because they were harassed and helpless, like sheep without a shepherd. Then he said to his disciples: 'The harvest is plentiful, but the labourers are few; therefore ask the Lord of the harvest to send out labourers into his harvest.' Then Jesus summoned his twelve disciples and gave them authority over unclean spirits, to cast them out, and to cure every disease and every sickness. He said: 'But go rather to the lost sheep of the house of Israel. As you go, proclaim the good news, the kingdom of heaven has come near. Cure the sick, raise the dead, cleanse the lepers, cast out demons. You received without payment; give without payment.'

Prayer

Be with me Lord when I need strength and healing in my life;
Be with your people so that we may follow you in loving service.
Be with our world in its need for your mercy and your care. Amen.

Reflection

This seems a really outgoing gospel. We are to look at the big harvest, the sick, the dead, the outcasts; all the needs of people are part of prayer. In care and compassion, the kingdom of heaven comes near. Prayer is one door into the kingdom of heaven, with a door outwards to the world of great need. Advent is a time to notice and to respond to the needs of people in our immediate circle as well in the wider world.

2nd Sunday of Advent: A

Matthew 3:1-12
In those days John the Baptist appeared in the wilderness of Judea, proclaiming: 'Repent, for the kingdom of heaven has come near.' This is the one of whom the prophet Isaiah spoke when he said: 'The voice of one crying out in the wilderness: "Prepare the way of the Lord, make his paths straight".' Now John wore clothing of camel's hair with a leather belt around his waist, and his food was locusts and wild honey. Then the people of Jerusalem and all Judea were going out to him, and all the region along the Jordan, and they were baptised by him in the river Jordan, confessing their sins. But when he saw many Pharisees and Sadducees coming for baptism, he said to them: 'You brood of vipers! Who warned you to flee from the wrath to come? Bear fruit worthy of repentance. Do not presume to say to yourselves: "We have Abraham as our ancestor", for I tell you, God is able from these stones to raise up children to Abraham. Even now the axe is lying at the root of the trees; every tree therefore that does not bear good fruit is cut down and thrown into the fire. I baptise you with water for repentance, but one who is more powerful than I is coming after me; I am not worthy to carry his sandals. He will baptise

you with the Holy Spirit and fire. His winnowing-fork is in his hand, and he will clear his threshing-floor and will gather his wheat into the granary; but the chaff he will burn with unquenchable fire.'

Prayer
May your coming among us this year, Lord God, open our hearts to your love,
and to your call to share your love among those we love, care for and meet each day.
May your love be upon us, O Lord as we place all our hope in you.

Reflection
The publicity and preaching of John the Baptist announces the hope of God's reign on earth coming nearer, the way of the Lord is being prepared. In a world of much despair – economic, political and violent, we need this message of hope. In a church which has been badly served by some who abused their power especially at the expense of the innocence of children, we welcome a message of repentant hope. In our own worried and anxieties about the future, about our children and about our old age, we want to be touched with hope. The hope is the sure and certain hope that God is always near, and promises life and love forever.

2nd Sunday of Advent: B

Mark 1:1-8

The beginning of the good news of Jesus Christ, the Son of God. As it is written in the prophet Isaiah: 'See, I am sending my messenger ahead of you, who will prepare your way the voice of one crying out in the wilderness: "Prepare the way of the Lord, make his paths straight".' John the baptiser appeared in the wilderness, proclaiming a baptism of repentance for the forgiveness of sins. And people from the whole Judean countryside and all the people of Jerusalem were going out to him, and were baptised by him in the river Jordan, confessing their sins. Now John was clothed with camel's hair, with a leather belt around his waist, and he ate locusts and wild honey. He proclaimed: 'The one who is more powerful than I is coming after me; I am not worthy to stoop down and untie the thong of his sandals. I have baptised you with water; but he will baptise you with the Holy Spirit.'

Prayer

May your coming among us this year, Lord God, open our hearts to your love,
and to your call to share your love among those we love, care for and meet each day.
May your love be upon us, O Lord as we place all our hope in you.

Reflection

John the Baptist preached forgiveness. This is one of the special gifts of God, and one of the big celebrations of Advent. We are a forgiven people, and we welcome the forgiveness of God in our repentance. This means we are firstly grateful for forgiveness, that we do not have to carry forever the burden of sin, meanness and our faults and failings. God covers them over in mercy. The second step of welcoming forgiveness is to try to do better in life – to move on from this sinfulness and meanness to a life of care, compassion, love and joy, and to make steps to forgive others.

2nd Sunday of Advent: C

Luke 3:1-6

In the fifteenth year of the reign of Emperor Tiberius, when Pontius Pilate was governor of Judea, and Herod was ruler of Galilee, and his brother Philip ruler of the region of Ituraea and Trachonitis, and Lysanias ruler of Abilene, during the high-priesthood of Annas and Caiaphas, the word of God came to John son of Zechariah in the wilderness. He went into all the region around the Jordan, proclaiming a baptism of repentance for the forgiveness of sins, as it is written in the book of the words of the prophet Isaiah,

> The voice of one crying out in the wilderness:
> 'Prepare the way of the Lord,
> make his paths straight.
> Every valley shall be filled,
> and every mountain and hill shall be made low,
> and the crooked shall be made straight,
> and the rough ways made smooth;
> and all flesh shall see the salvation of God.

Prayer

May your coming among us this year, Lord God, open our hearts to your love,
and to your call to share your love among those we love, care for and meet each day.
May your love be upon us, O Lord as we place all our hope in you. Amen.

Reflection

In a poem about her life an old lady wrote: 'I would wear purple more often.' To remind her that life can be different day by day, or that she might be personally noticed and change her life. We can immerse ourselves in the mood of waiting for Christmas, and take this on the spiritual level and well as the ordinary. All of the weeks of Advent can be a preparation for the way of the Lord, which we will hear of during the readings of the coming year. This is a time of joyful waiting, knowing we cannot be let down. The purple of Advent is not the purple of mourning but of joyful anticipation. It's like we dress in the football teams colours early in the morning to look forward to a match.

Week 2: Monday

Luke 5:12-17

One day, while he was teaching, Pharisees and teachers of the law were sitting nearby (they had come from every village of Galilee and Judea and from Jerusalem); and the power of the Lord was with him to heal. Just then some men came, carrying a paralysed man on a bed. They were trying to bring him in and lay him before Jesus; but finding no way to bring him in because of the crowd, they went up on the roof and let him down with his bed through the tiles into the middle of the crowd in front of Jesus. When he saw their faith, he said: 'Friend, your sins are forgiven you.' Then the scribes and the Pharisees began to question: 'Who is this who is speaking blasphemies? Who can forgive sins but God alone?' When Jesus perceived their questionings, he answered them: 'Why do you raise such questions in your hearts? Which is easier, to say: "Your sins are forgiven you", or to say, "Stand up and walk"? But so that you may know that the Son of Man has authority on earth to forgive sins' – he said to the one who was paralysed – "I say to you, stand up and take your bed and go to your home." Immediately he stood up before them, took what he had been lying on, and went to his home, glorifying God. Amazement seized all of them, and they glorified God and were filled with awe, saying: 'We have seen strange things today.'

Prayer
May your coming among us this year, Lord God, open our hearts to your love,
and to your call to share your love among those we love, care for and meet each day.
May your love be upon us, O Lord, as we place all our hope in you.

Reflection
A forgotten person in this gospel story is the man who owned the house and whose roof was now destroyed. Perhaps he felt privileged to help Jesus, or annoyed at damage; perhaps they all helped him repair the roof. We don't know – but we do know that if we allow Jesus deeply into our lives, something will change. Jesus means big changes on how we look on others, as well as how we look on ourselves. Advent prepares us for the Christmas revolution – that all are loved, and the least in the world are the greatest with God.

Week 2: Tuesday

Matthew 18:12-14
Jesus said to his disciples: 'What do you think? If a man has a hundred sheep, and one of them has gone astray, does he not leave the ninety-nine on the hills and go in search of the one that went astray? And if he finds it, truly I say to you, he rejoices over it more than over the ninety-nine that never went astray. So it is not the will of my father who is in heaven that one of these little ones should perish.'

Prayer

May your coming among us this year, Lord God, open our hearts to your love,
and to your call to share your love among those we love, care for and meet each day.
May your love be upon us, O Lord as we place all our hope in you. Amen.

Reflection

We are the little ones. We are little at prayer – little in what we are in the sight of God because all we are and have is from God. God wants us to be at our best, our most alive. He wants nothing good in us to perish. Nothing good we have done or have tried to do is wasted. All is valued in the mind and heart of God, and we are saved, honoured and loved by the One who creates us each day. Advent reminds us of what it is like to be a little one, dependent on others and God for so much in life.

Week 2: Wednesday

Matthew 11:28-30
Jesus said: 'Come to me, all you that are weary and are carrying heavy burdens, and I will give you rest. Take my yoke upon you, and learn from me; for I am gentle and humble in heart, and you will find rest for your souls. For my yoke is easy, and my burden is light.'

A Nurse's Prayer

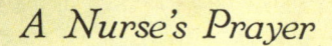

O my God, teach me to receive the sick in Thy Name. Give to my efforts success for the glory of Thy holy Name.

It is Thy work: without Thee, I cannot succeed.

Grant that the sick Thou hast placed in my care may be abundantly blessed, and not one of them be lost because of any neglect on my part.

Help me to overcome every temporal weakness, and strengthen in me whatever may enable me to bring joy to the lives of those I serve.

Give me grace, for the sake of Thy sick ones and of those lives that will be influenced by them.

Amen.

Prayer

May your coming among us this year, Lord God, open our hearts to your love,
and to your call to share your love among those we love, care for and meet each day.
May your love be upon us, O Lord as we place all our hope in you. Amen.

Reflection

Christmas can be busy. Preparations, social and other can keep us very stressed. Advent is the time to come and rest, to find comfort and peace in our God. Some cultures hype Christmas so much that it is almost over-celebrated before the middle of December. The weeks of Advent are the invitation from God to find security, depth and peace in belonging to him. Our mutual belonging is seen in the God-child of Advent, Jesus the Christ.

Week 2: Thursday

Matthew 11:11-15

Jesus said: 'Truly I tell you, among those born of women no one has arisen greater than John the Baptist; yet the least in the kingdom of heaven is greater than he. From the days of John the Baptist until now the kingdom of heaven has suffered violence, and the violent take it by force. For all the prophets and the law prophesied until John came; and if you are willing to accept it, he is Elijah who is to come. Let anyone with ears listen'.

Prayer

May your coming among us this year, Lord God, open our hearts to your love,
and to your call to share your love among those we love, care for and meet each day.
May your love be upon us, O Lord as we place all our hope in you. Amen.

Reflection

Jesus is not a man on his own for God. He has been expected and his life is intertwined with the prophets and with John the Baptist. Later it would be with his apostles, with the men and women who accompanied him on his mission. Our Christian life is intertwined also with the community of the followers of Jesus. Friends, co-workers, family, the wider church – all are part of everyone's journey with Jesus to God. Our Advent prayer is a prayer that welcomes into our lives the people God sends across our path – whom we will help lead to him, and who help lead each of us to him.

Week 2: Friday

Matthew 11:16-19

Jesus spoke to the crowds: 'But to what will I compare this generation? It is like children sitting in the marketplaces and calling to one another: "We played the flute for you, and you did not dance; we wailed, and you did not mourn." For John came neither eating nor drinking, and they say: "He has a demon"; the Son of Man came eating and drinking, and they say: "Look, a glutton and a drunkard, a friend of tax collectors and sinners!" Yet wisdom is vindicated by her deeds.'

Prayer

May your coming among us this year, Lord God, open our hearts to your love,
and to your call to share your love among those we love, care for and meet each day.
May your love be upon us, O Lord as we place all our hope in you. Amen.

Reflection

When we don't like what's going on, don't we sometimes misjudge people? Or we put on them what we don't like about ourselves. Jesus looks more at what people do for each other than what others may say about them. This is not an easy piece of the gospel to pray. But if we focus on John and Jesus, we can go beyond what people say of them to what they say of themselves and what their deeds were like: the blind could see, the lame could walk and freedom was the gift to the human heart.

Week 2: Saturday

Matthew 17:10-13

And the disciples asked him: 'Why, then, do the scribes say that Elijah must come first? ' He replied: 'Elijah is indeed coming and will restore all things; but I tell you that Elijah has already come, and they did not recognise him, but they did to him whatever they pleased. So also the Son of Man is about to suffer at their hands.' Then the disciples understood that he was speaking to them about John the Baptist.

Prayer

May your coming among us this year, Lord God, open our hearts to your love,
and to your call to share your love among those we love, care for and meet each day.
May your love be upon us, O Lord as we place all our hope in you. Amen.

Reflection

This child soon to come will soon suffer. 'Babe so soon to be nailed to a tree', in the words of a recent carol. The eastern icons of Christmas sometimes have the manger in the form of a coffin. The crib is at its most realistic when the cross is somewhere in the background. All his life Jesus was aware that he would suffer; and not alone he himself, but John the Baptist and all who would follow him. The following of Jesus will challenge us on all the areas of our life – how we love, how we treat the poor and needy, and how we give some time in our lives to God and the things of God.

3rd Sunday of Advent: A

Matthew 11:2-11
Now when Jesus had finished instructing his twelve disciples, he went on from there to teach and proclaim his message in their cities.

When John heard in prison what the Messiah was doing, he sent word by his disciples and said to him: 'Are you the one who is to come, or are we to wait for another?' Jesus answered them: 'Go and tell John what you hear and see: the blind receive their sight, the lame walk, the lepers are cleansed, the deaf hear, the dead are raised, and the poor have good news brought to them. And blessed is anyone who takes no offence at me.'

As they went away, Jesus began to speak to the crowds about John: 'What did you go out into the wilderness to look at? A reed shaken by the wind? What then did you go out to see? Someone dressed in soft robes? Look, those who wear soft robes are in royal palaces. What then did you go out to see? A prophet? Yes, I tell you, and more than a prophet. This is the one about whom it is written,

> See, I am sending my messenger ahead of you,
> who will prepare your way before you.

Truly I tell you, among those born of

women no one has arisen greater than John the Baptist; yet the least in the kingdom of heaven is greater than he.'

Prayer
Come Lord and save us – save us from the evil that can be part of our world;
save us from the evil in our hearts.
Fill the spaces of our heart and the heart of the world
with love, peace, reconciliation and the joy of your birth. Amen.

Reflection
We live in a world that is not equal for everyone; we live in a city where we may not know poverty exists as much as it does. The gospel says that the healing of the sick and the improvement of life are signs of Jesus. Christianity is a very social gospel. You don't see much of Jesus on his own, except at prayer. We don't go to God or find God on our own.

We find God in our helping those in need, specially those most in need in our society and world.

3rd Sunday of Advent: B

John 1:6-8, 19-28

There was a man sent from God, whose name was John. He came as a witness to testify to the light, so that all might believe through him. He himself was not the light, but he came to testify to the light. This is the testimony given by John when the Jews sent priests and Levites from Jerusalem to ask him: 'Who are you?' He confessed and did not deny it, but confessed: 'I am not the Messiah.' And they asked him: 'What then? Are you Elijah?' He said: 'I am not.' 'Are you the prophet?' He answered: 'No.' Then they said to him: 'Who are you? Let us have an answer for those who sent us. What do you say about yourself?' He said: 'I am the voice of one crying out in the wilderness: "Make straight the way of the Lord" as the prophet Isaiah said.' Now they had been sent from the Pharisees. They asked him: 'Why then are you baptising if you are neither the Messiah, nor Elijah, nor the prophet?' John answered them: 'I baptise with water. Among you stands one whom you do not know, the one who is to come.'

Prayer

Come Lord and save us – save us from the evil that can be part of our world;
save us from the evil in our hearts.
Fill the spaces of our heart and the heart of the world
with love, peace, reconciliation and the joy of your birth. Amen.

Reflection

Christmas is not meant to be quiet. It's meant to explode with the roar of the crowd when its team gets the score. It's meant to laugh with the joy of parents whose child has just been born. It's meant to be a voice of care, compassion and love, the voice of God, in the wilderness of the world. This could be a week of active expectancy – to do something to prepare well for the Lord. Do something for the poor each day, thank somebody genuinely each day for their place in your life, approach the communal sacrament of Penance (Reconciliation) or go to confession privately, go to Mass once or twice more in the week, say sorry to someone you hurt or forgive someone who hurt you. Then the Lord will not take us by surprise, then the One who is coming among us will not be unknown, then we will have a fuller Christmas and because of each one, someone else will have a happier Christmas.

3rd Sunday of Advent: C

Luke 3:10-18
And the crowds asked him: 'What then should we do?' In reply he said to them: 'Whoever has two coats must share with anyone who has none; and whoever has food must do likewise.' Even tax-collectors came to be baptised, and they asked him: 'Teacher, what should we do?' He said to them: 'Collect no more than the amount prescribed for you.' Soldiers also asked him: 'And we, what should we do?' He said to them: 'Do not extort money from anyone by threats or false accusation, and be satisfied with your wages.' As the people were filled with expectation, and all were questioning in their hearts concerning John, whether he might be the Messiah, John answered all of them by saying: 'I baptise you with water; but one who is more powerful than I is coming; I am not worthy to untie the thong of his sandals. He will baptise you with the Holy Spirit and fire. His winnowing-fork is in his hand, to clear his threshing-floor and to gather the wheat into his granary; but the chaff he will burn with unquenchable fire. So, with many other exhortations, he proclaimed the good news to the people.

Prayer:

Come Lord and save us – save us from the evil that can be part of our world;
save us from the evil in our hearts.
Fill the spaces of our heart and the heart of the world
with love, peace, reconciliation and the joy of your birth. Amen.

Reflection

This mid-point of Advent alerts us to issues of justice and equality. The prophet John has been asked as a sort of trick by people who exploited others with tax bills, and soldiers who often used their brute force on others, how they should repent. His words were tough but quite ordinary – don't overcharge, share your surplus with the needy and don't exploit people. Another way, a bit more figurative, of stating the basic demands of 'Love one another'.

Week 3: Monday

Matthew 21:23-27
When Jesus entered the temple, the chief priests and the elders of the people came to him as he was teaching, and said: 'By what authority are you doing these things, and who gave you this authority? 'Jesus said to them: 'I will also ask you one question; if you tell me the answer, then I will also tell you by what authority I do these things. Did the baptism of John come from heaven, or was it of human origin? ' And they argued with one another: 'If we say, "From heaven", he will say to us, "Why then did you not believe him?" But if we say: "Of human origin", we are afraid of the crowd; for all regard John as a prophet. 'So they answered Jesus: 'We do not know. ' And he said to them: 'Neither will I tell you by what authority I am doing these things.'

Prayer

Come Lord and save us – save us from the evil that can be part of our world;
save us from the evil in our hearts.
Fill the spaces of our heart and the heart of the world
with love, peace, reconciliation and the joy of your birth. Amen.

Reflection

There is a big mystery about Jesus. Where he came from, why he does what he does – all made people think, doubt, get confused or find faith. He wants us to mull over his life, savour it, even take our doubts seriously. Prayer is our daily insertion – personal or communal – into the mystery of the life and the purpose of Jesus in his life on earth. In him heaven and earth are mingled. In prayer heaven mingles with earth. This happens also in love – our prayer is to be fruitful in a loving life.

Week 3: Tuesday

Matthew 21:28-32
Jesus said: 'What do you think? A man had two sons; he went to the first and said: 'Son, go and work in the vineyard today.' He answered: 'I will not' but later he changed his mind and went. The father went to the second and said the same; and he answered: 'I go, sir', but he did not go. Which of the two did the will of his father?'They said: 'The first.' Jesus said to them: 'Truly I tell you, the tax collectors and the prostitutes are going into the kingdom of God ahead of you. For John came to you in the way of righteousness and you did not believe him, but the tax collectors and the prostitutes believed him; and even after you saw it, you did not change your minds and believe him.'

Prayer

Come Lord and save us – save us from the evil that can be part of our world;
save us from the evil in our hearts.
Fill the spaces of our heart and the heart of the world
with love, peace, reconciliation and the joy of your birth. Amen.

Reflection

The gospel calls to faith. Faith builds on trust. We are challenged to believe, as people were to believe in John and Jesus. Faith grows and waxes and wanes. Trust is difficult; and we are called to total trust. Not just a bit here and there. Prayer can grow trust in us; human love does the same. In prayer we can thank God for those we trust and who trust each of us. In prayer we bring that area of self to God where we need to trust. Prayer a daily dose of trust in God!

Week 3: Wednesday

Luke 7:18-23
The disciples of John reported all these things to him. So John summoned two of his disciples and sent them to the Lord to ask: 'Are you the one who is to come, or are we to wait for another?' When the men had come to him, they said: 'John the Baptist has sent us to you to ask: "Are you the one who is to come, or are we to wait for another?"' Jesus had just then cured many people of diseases, plagues, and evil spirits, and had given sight to many who were blind. And he answered them: 'Go and tell John what you have seen and heard: the blind receive their sight, the lame walk, the lepers are cleansed, the deaf hear, the dead are raised, the poor have good news brought to them. And blessed is anyone who takes no offence at me.'

Prayer

Come Lord and save us – save us from the evil that can be part of our world;
save us from the evil in our hearts.
Fill the spaces of our heart and the heart of the world
with love, peace, reconciliation and the joy of your birth. Amen.

Reflection

The healing work of Jesus brought many to believe in him. But many others had to let go of their hopes of a political leader, a powerful one to free people from oppression. Jesus' hands are tied by the greed and sin of people, as he would be nailed to the cross. Much of human suffering is caused by others. Jesus is the one who accompanies us in time of need, holding a hand and healing the pain of anxiety, worry and doubt.

Week 3: Thursday

Luke 7:24-30
When John's messengers had gone, Jesus began to speak to the crowds about John: 'What did you go out into the wilderness to look at? A reed shaken by the wind? What then did you go out to see? Someone dressed in soft robes? Look, those who put on fine clothing and live in luxury are in royal palaces. What then did you go out to see? A prophet? Yes, I tell you, and more than a prophet. This is the one about whom it is written:

> See, I am sending my messenger ahead of you,
> who will prepare your way before you.

I tell you, among those born of women no one is greater than John; yet the least in the kingdom of God is greater than he.'

Prayer

Come Lord and save us – save us from the evil that can be part of our world;
save us from the evil in our hearts.
Fill the spaces of our heart and the heart of the world
with love, peace, reconciliation and the joy of your birth. Amen.

Reflection

We are still in the atmosphere this week of something about to happen. Like when the whole football stadium hushes while a free is taken, maybe to decide a match or a penalty shoot out to decide a world cup qualifier. John the Baptist is still on the scene, pointing where to look, where to wait, how to expect the one who is to come. Many reminders of Christmas are around . Let the them all – religious or secular – bring us into the flow of love in the world that is from God.

Week 3: Friday

John 5:33-36
Jesus said to the people: 'You sent messengers to John, and he testified to the truth. Not that I accept such human testimony, but I say these things so that you may be saved. He was a burning and shining lamp, and you were willing to rejoice for a while in his light. But I have a testimony greater than John's. The works that the Father has given me to complete, the very works that I am doing, testify on my behalf that the Father has sent me. And the Father who sent me has himself testified on my behalf. You have never heard his voice or seen his form, and you do not have his word abiding in you, because you do not believe him whom he has sent.'

Prayer

Come Lord and save us – save us from the evil that can be part of our world;
save us from the evil in our hearts.
Fill the spaces of our heart and the heart of the world
with love, peace, reconciliation and the joy of your birth. Amen.

Reflection

John, a man of faith, found this faith tested by Jesus. He was still wondering who the Messiah would be? John was a man with a lot of conviction and of truth. He preached a lot. We get an impression he could be a very strong preacher, and believed what he said. But he missed the point sometimes. He seemed to miss that Jesus would be found in helping others: the blind would see, the lame walk and the poor be looked after. Was he sometimes so concerned with reforming others that he could miss Jesus? But his trust that he would know the Messiah was strong and in this Jesus praised him.

17 December

Matthew 1:1-17

The book of the genealogy of Jesus Christ, the son of David, the son of Abraham. Abraham was the father of Isaac, and Isaac the father of Jacob, and Jacob the father of Judah and his brothers, ... and Matthan the father of Jacob, and Jacob the father of Joseph the husband of Mary, of whom Jesus was born, who is called Christ. So all the generations from Abraham to David were fourteen generations, and from David to the deportation to Babylon fourteen generations, and from the deportation to Babylon to the Christ fourteen generations.

Prayer:

Come Lord and save us – save us from the evil that can be part of our world;
save us from the evil in our hearts.
Fill the spaces of our heart and the heart of the world
with love, peace, reconciliation and the joy of your birth. Amen.

Reflection

You are a brave person to pray this gospel! It is mostly omitted when we find it at Mass, and unless we know something of the background, it makes little sense. The list is placing Jesus in the mainstream of human life and his people. It lists all sorts of people, holy and not so holy, public sinners, outcasts and the type of people you wouldn't associate with. In our family tree we might erase them or pretend they never existed. The list God's list of favourites and of co-workers. All can be partners with God in the coming of the kingdom, that includes me and you, and all sort of people you might normally not invite to dinner or coffee.

18 December

Matthew 1:18-25

Now the birth of Jesus the Messiah took place in this way. When his mother Mary had been engaged to Joseph, but before they lived together, she was found to be with child from the Holy Spirit. Her husband Joseph, being a righteous man and unwilling to expose her to public disgrace, planned to dismiss her quietly. But just when he had resolved to do this, an angel of the Lord appeared to him in a dream and said: 'Joseph, son of David, do not be afraid to take Mary as your wife, for the child conceived in her is from the Holy Spirit. She will bear a son, and you are to name him Jesus, for he will save his people from their sins.' All this took place to fulfill what had been spoken by the Lord through the prophet:

Look, the virgin shall conceive and bear a son, and they shall name him Emmanuel,

which means, 'God is with us.' When Joseph awoke from sleep, he did as the angel of the Lord commanded him; he took her as his wife, but had no marital relations with her until she had borne a son; and he named him Jesus.

Prayer

Come Lord and save us – save us from the evil that can be part of our world;
save us from the evil in our hearts.

Fill the spaces of our heart and the heart of the world
with love, peace, reconciliation and the joy of your birth. Amen.

Reflection

Advent is seldom seen as a time of the Hoy Spirit, but in the annunciation to Joseph, and to Mary earlier, the Spirit is alive and at work. In a mysterious, miraculous way, known only in faith, the Spirit's action brings to the world the God-person, the human in the divine and the divine in the human in a totally physical and spiritual way. In the humanity of Mary, Jesus is growing, from embryo to child. In the faith of Joseph, the call first come to all of us to believe the mystery. In prayer we might picture Mary and Joseph talking together about all that has happened and picture the holy Spirit in the air, in the love and in the atmosphere around them. Bring that presence of the Spirit into your day today.

19 December

From Luke 1:5-25

In the days of King Herod of Judea, there was a priest named Zechariah, who belonged to the priestly order of Abijah. His wife was a descendant of Aaron, and her name was Elizabeth. Both of them were righteous before God, living blamelessly according to all the commandments and regulations of the Lord. But they had no children, because Elizabeth was barren, and both were getting on in years. Once when he was serving as priest before God and his section was on duty, he was chosen by lot, according to the custom of the priesthood, to enter the sanctuary of the Lord and offer incense. Now at the time of the incense-offering, the whole assembly of the people was praying outside. Then there appeared to him an angel of the Lord, standing at the right side of the altar of incense. When Zechariah saw him, he was terrified; and fear overwhelmed him. But the angel said to him: 'Do not be afraid, Zechariah, for your prayer has been heard. Your wife Elizabeth will bear you a son, and you will name him John.'

Prayer

Come, Lord Jesus, save your people.
Save us from the evil and less good sides of ourselves;
Save us from the greed and corruption of our world.
Save us in your love, care and compassion,
Child of God, child of Mary. Amen.

Reflection

Zechariah was speechless through lack of faith. His obstinacy to believe made him isolated and like an island among his family and fellow-priests. Faith draws us into communion with many others, of all faiths and churches. We share much in faith, and forge links which bind us in prayer, support and friendship. Zechariah was never deserted by God; with the birth of John his faith and speech returned. A child may often bring us to faith where faith is missing. Watch a child today, think of a child today, remember childhood today, and be close to life, to mystery and to God!

20 December

Luke 1: 26-38

In the sixth month the angel Gabriel was sent by God to a town in Galilee called Nazareth, to a virgin engaged to a man whose name was Joseph, of the house of David. The virgin's name was Mary. And he came to her and said: 'Greetings, favoured one! The Lord is with you.' But she was much perplexed by his words and pondered what sort of greeting this might be. The angel said to her: 'Do not be afraid, Mary, for you have found favour with God. And now, you will conceive in your womb and bear a son, and you will name him Jesus. He will be great, and will be called the Son of the Most High, and the Lord God will give to him the throne of his ancestor David. He will reign over the house of Jacob forever, and of his kingdom there will be no end.' Mary said to the angel: 'How can this be, since I am a virgin?' The angel said to her: 'The Holy Spirit will come upon you, and the power of the Most High will overshadow you; therefore the child to be born will be holy; he will be called Son of God. And now, your relative Elizabeth in her old age has also conceived a son; and this is the sixth month for her who was said to be barren. For nothing will be impossible with God.' Then Mary said: 'Here am I, the servant of the Lord;

let it be with me according to your word.' Then the angel departed from her.

Prayer

Come, Lord Jesus, save your people.
Save us from the evil and less good sides of ourselves;
Save us from the greed and corruption of our world.
Save us in your love, care and compassion,
Child of God, child of Mary. Amen.

Reflection

Emmanuel – a mantra for Advent and Christmas prayer. If we speak it from the heart we are in touch with God who is near. In our faith in the mystery – Emmanuel, God is with us – we are close to God who is present in our hearts. God is as near as the air we breathe,. With each breath in prayer, just say 'Emmanuel'. It is our Christmas welcome to the child who is our God.

Week 4: Sunday: A

Matthew 1: 18-25

Now the birth of Jesus the Messiah took place in this way. When his mother Mary had been engaged to Joseph, but before they lived together, she was found to be with child from the Holy Spirit. Her husband Joseph, being a righteous man and unwilling to expose her to public disgrace, planned to dismiss her quietly. But just when he had resolved to do this, an angel of the Lord appeared to him in a dream and said: 'Joseph, son of David, do not be afraid to take Mary as your wife, for the child conceived in her is from the Holy Spirit. She will bear a son, and you are to name him Jesus, for he will save his people from their sins.' All this took place to fulfill what had been spoken by the Lord through the prophet:

> Look, the virgin shall conceive and bear a son,
> and they shall name him Emmanuel,

which means, 'God is with us.' When Joseph awoke from sleep, he did as the angel of the Lord commanded him; he took her as his wife, but had no marital relations with her until she had borne a son; and he named him Jesus.

Prayer

Come, Lord Jesus, save your people.
Save us from the evil and less good sides of ourselves;
Save us from the greed and corruption of our world.
Save us in your love, care and compassion,
Child of God, child of Mary. Amen.

Reflection

People wondered in Old Testament times how they would build a house for God. Later we would learn that the house would be the body or Mary and the house would be all of us. It changes our view of others – God is in all of us. We can ignore that, or we can help God be found in all of us. God is often deeply hidden, and God is active through each of us for each other.

Week 4: Sunday: B

Luke 1:26-38
In the sixth month the angel Gabriel was sent by God to a town in Galilee called Nazareth, to a virgin engaged to a man whose name was Joseph, of the house of David. The virgin's name was Mary. And he came to her and said: 'Greetings, favoured one! The Lord is with you. 'But she was much perplexed by his words and pondered what sort of greeting this might be. The angel said to her: 'Do not be afraid, Mary, for you have found favour with God. And now, you will conceive in your womb and bear a son, and you will name him Jesus. He will be great, and will be called the Son of the Most High, and the Lord God will give to him the throne of his ancestor David. He will reign over the house of Jacob forever, and of his kingdom there will be no end.' Mary said to the angel: 'How can this be, since I am a virgin?' The angel said to her: 'The Holy Spirit will come upon you, and the power of the Most High will overshadow you; therefore the child to be born will be holy; he will be called Son of God. And now, your relative Elizabeth in her old age has also conceived a son; and this is the sixth month for her who was said to be barren. For nothing will be impossible with God.' Then Mary said: 'Here am I, the servant of the Lord;

let it be with me according to your word.' Then the angel departed from her.

Prayer

Come, Lord Jesus, save your people.
Save us from the evil and less good sides of ourselves;
Save us from the greed and corruption of our world.
Save us in your love, care and compassion,
Child of God, child of Mary. Amen.

Reflection

Christmas highlights the belief that God is in all of us. God is often deeply hidden, and God is active through each of us for each other. In the visit of Mary, God came close to Elizabeth in the ordinary and homely moments of every day. Christmas and the Advent days give us the space to allow the huge eternal mystery become part of the everyday.

Week 4: Sunday: C

Luke 1:39-44

In those days Mary set out and went with haste to a Judean town in the hill country, where she entered the house of Zechariah and greeted Elizabeth. When Elizabeth heard Mary's greeting, the child leapt in her womb. And Elizabeth was filled with the Holy Spirit and exclaimed with a loud cry: 'Blessed are you among women, and blessed is the fruit of your womb. And why has this happened to me, that the mother of my Lord comes to me? For as soon as I heard the sound of your greeting, the child in my womb leapt for joy. And blessed is she who believed that there would be a fulfilment of what was spoken to her by the Lord.'

Prayer

Come, Lord Jesus, save your people.
Save us from the evil and less good sides of ourselves;
Save us from the greed and corruption of our world.
Save us in your love, care and compassion,
Child of God, child of Mary. Amen.

Reflection

One of Mary's first recorded journeys was after the announcement to her of being the mother of God. It was a journey of service, a visit to her cousin who needed help. A time when women wants another woman to talk to ... Get rid of the men, this is women's stuff. When we're going through something and others have had the same – like pregnancy, bereavement, redundancy, a son in prison, a daughter on drugs ... we want to talk, we want support. They had something else to share – their faith. The prayers they said have been said ever since. The stage was small but the audience has been millions ever since.

22 December

Luke 1:46-56

And Mary said: 'My soul magnifies the Lord, and my spirit rejoices in God my Saviour, for he has looked with favour on the lowliness of his servant. Surely, from now on all generations will call me blessed; for the Mighty One has done great things for me, and holy is his name. His mercy is for those who fear him from generation to generation. He has shown strength with his arm; he has scattered the proud in the thoughts of their hearts. He has brought down the powerful from their thrones, and lifted up the lowly; he has filled the hungry with good things, and sent the rich away empty. He has helped his servant Israel, in remembrance of his mercy, according to the promise he made to our ancestors, to Abraham and to his descendants forever.' And Mary remained with Elizabeth about three months and then returned to her home.

Prayer

Come, Lord Jesus, save your people.
Save us from the evil and less good sides of ourselves;
Save us from the greed and corruption of our world.
Save us in your love, care and compassion,
Child of God, child of Mary. Amen.

Reflection

Did you ever write your own Magnificat? In prayer you could notice the reasons you want to praise God yourself. The simplest of meetings with another can be manifestations of the divine. The simplest of winter or summer creation can touch us with the nearness of God. Emmanuel, God is with us, is the mantra of these days. Emmanuel is everywhere. All is a sacrament of God. Praise is a natural response to God; it wells up from the hidden depths of our hearts. Praise and thanks go hand in hand; praise for what is great, thanks for what is ordinary.

23 December

Luke 1:57-66

Now the time came for Elizabeth to give birth, and she bore a son. Her neighbours and relatives heard that the Lord had shown his great mercy to her, and they rejoiced with her. On the eighth day they came to circumcise the child, and they were going to name him Zechariah after his father. But his mother said: 'No; he is to be called John.' They said to her: 'None of your relatives has this name.' Then they began motioning to his father to find out what name he wanted to give him. He asked for a writing tablet and wrote: 'His name is John. ' And all of them were amazed. Immediately his mouth was opened and his tongue freed, and he began to speak, praising God. Fear came over all their neighbours, and all these things were talked about throughout the entire hill country of Judea. All who heard them pondered them and said: 'What then will this child become?' For, indeed, the hand of the Lord was with him.

Prayer

Come, Lord Jesus, save your people.
Save us from the evil and less good sides of ourselves;
Save us from the greed and corruption of our world.
Save us in your love, care and compassion,
Child of God, child of Mary. Amen.

Reflection

We know the end of the story which begins in the early gospel of Luke. We know what this child will become – the announcer of the Lord and the one who would be martyred and beheaded by the evil of Herod. We know too that the one he announces would be killed also, but would rise again. We may know too much; we may be burdened with the knowledge of so much evil affecting these men's lives. We ask in prayer that our knowledge flow from head to heart, so that our lives may follow the love which each of these children would live by.

24 December

Luke 1:67-79

Then his father Zechariah was filled with the Holy Spirit and spoke this prophecy: 'Blessed be the Lord God of Israel, for he has looked favourably on his people and redeemed them. He has raised up a mighty saviour for us in the house of his servant David, as he spoke through the mouth of his holy prophets from of old, that we would be saved from our enemies and from the hand of all who hate us. Thus he has shown the mercy promised to our ancestors, and has remembered his holy covenant, the oath that he swore to our ancestor Abraham, to grant us that we, being rescued from the hands of our enemies, might serve him without fear, in holiness and righteousness before him all our days. And you, child, will be called the prophet of the Most High; for you will go before the Lord to prepare his ways, to give knowledge of salvation to his people by the forgiveness of their sins. By the tender mercy of our God, the dawn from on high will break upon us, to give light to those who sit in darkness and in the shadow of death, to guide our feet into the way of peace. '

Prayer

Come, Lord Jesus, save your people.
Save us from the evil and less good sides of ourselves;
Save us from the greed and corruption of our world.
Save us in your love, care and compassion,
Child of God, child of Mary. Amen.

Reflection

Allow this psalm of thanks and praise be made for you. Zechariah made this prayer for his son. It was a prayer grown and made in love. We are now the ones who go before the Lord; our love and care can be the dawn breaking into the lives of others, giving light to all in darkness. We are the ones to walk with the peace that calms and guides others on their journey. Take what is suitable from this great prayer, said each morning in the church, and allow it link you with the living Christ.

25 December

The Nativity of Our Lord

John 1:1-5, 9-14
In the beginning was the Word, and the Word was with God, and the Word was God. He was in the beginning with God. All things came into being through him, and without him not one thing came into being. What has come into being in him was life, and the life was the light of all people. The light shines in the darkness, and the darkness did not overcome it. The true light, which enlightens everyone, was coming into the world.

He was in the world, and the world came into being through him; yet the world did not know him. He came to what was his own, and his own people did not accept him. But to all who received him, who believed in his name, he gave power to become children of God, who were born, not of blood or of the will of the flesh or of the will of man, but of God.

And the Word became flesh and lived among us, and we have seen his glory, the glory as of a father's only son, full of grace and truth.

Prayer

Come, Lord Jesus, save your people.
Save us from the evil and less good sides of ourselves;
Save us from the greed and corruption of our world.
Save us in your love, care and compassion,
Child of God, child of Mary,
Born this day in Bethlehem,
Born this day among us. Amen.

Reflection

No love that in a family dwells,
No carolling in frosty air,
Nor all the steeple-shaking bells
Can with this single Truth compare –
That God was Man in Palestine
And lives today in Bread and Wine.
G. K. Chesterton

December 8

Luke 1:26-38
In the sixth month the angel Gabriel was sent by God to a town in Galilee called Nazareth, to a virgin engaged to a man whose name was Joseph, of the house of David. The virgin's name was Mary. And he came to her and said: 'Greetings, favoured one! The Lord is with you.' But she was much perplexed by his words and pondered what sort of greeting this might be. The angel said to her: 'Do not be afraid, Mary, for you have found favour with God. And now, you will conceive in your womb and bear a son, and you will name him Jesus. He will be great, and will be called the Son of the Most High, and the Lord God will give to him the throne of his ancestor David. He will reign over the house of Jacob forever, and of his kingdom there will be no end.' Mary said to the angel: 'How can this be, since I am a virgin?' The angel said to her: 'The Holy Spirit will come upon you, and the power of the Most High will overshadow you; therefore the child to be born will be holy; he will be called Son of God. And now, your relative Elizabeth in her old age has also conceived a son; and this is the sixth month for her who was said to be barren. For nothing will be impossible with God.' Then Mary said: 'Here am I, the servant of the Lord;

let it be with me according to your word.' Then the angel departed from her.

Prayer

Mary, woman of faith, pray for us.
Mary, called into the love of the trinity, pray for us.
Mary, mother of Jesus,
Son of God and one of us,
Pray for, sinners,
Now and at the hour of our death. Amen.

Reflection

The world would never be the same because of Mary's 'yes' to the invitation to be the mother of God. Because of Mary, God is with us in a totally new way in the world, in the person of the human and divine Jesus. Later in their lives, Jesus would praise Mary not just for being the physical mother, but because she 'heard the word of God and kept it'. She kept the word of God close to her heart, as she kept the body of Jesus close to herself in her womb, in her family life and always. In prayer we may ask her to bring the word of God to life in us, as the word became flesh in her.